The Story of a Special Day
Volume 332

November

27

The 331st day of the year (332nd in leap years).
There are 34 days remaining until the end of the year.

by Michael Dobson

Timespinner
Press

This book is also available in e-book form for Kindle, e-pub devices, and other formats from your favorite online booksellers.

For more information about the series, about us, or about your special day, please email us at editor@timespinnerpress.com.

Look for other volumes in *The Story of a Special Day,* coming often. See www.timespinnerpress.com for details and for the most recent information.

Table of Contents

For the definition of "O.S.," "CE," and "BCE" used with some dates , see the section "On Names and Dates."

Quote of the Day

"Faith makes it possible to achieve that which man's mind can conceive and believe."

Bruce Lee, martial artist
born November 27, 1940

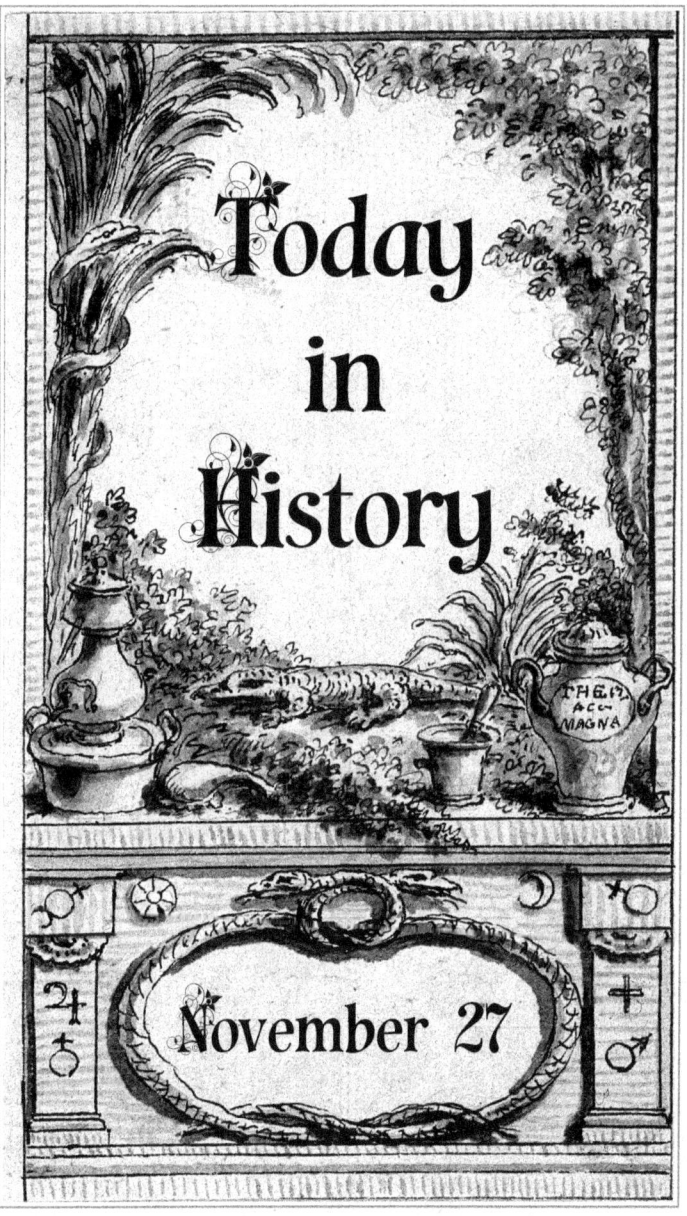

Today in History

November 27

Mr. Potato Head balloon at the 2007 Macy's Thanskgiving Day
Parade (Photo: Ian Gampon, CC BY-SA 2.0)

Event of the Day
Macy's Thanksgiving Day Parade

On November 27, 1924, the first Macy's Thanksgiving Day Parade took place in New York City..

The predominantly first-generation immigrant staff of Macy's department store chain, proud of their new American heritage, wanted to celebrate the American Thanksgiving holiday with a street festival. Macy's was then in the process of acquiring New Jersey's Bamberger's department store, and so transferred the annual Bamberger's Thanksgiving Day parade to New York City. Dressed in costumes, Macy's and Bamberger's employees marched to the flagship Macy's store on 34th Street, accompanied by floats, bands, and animals borrowed from the Central Park Zoo. At the very end of the parade, Santa Claus arrived, where he was placed on a throne on the Macy's balcony and crowned "Kind of the Kiddies."

That first Macy's Thanksgiving Day parade attracted over 250,000 people, and Macy's declared the parade would be an annual event. Except for the World War II years of 1942-1944, the parade has been held each year since 1924. Television broadcasts of the parade began in 1939. Today, millions of people line the parade route to watch the event live, and well over 44 million people watch the parade on television.

The use of live animals in the parade quickly gave way to the famous giant balloons for which the Macy's Day parade is famous. Marionette creator Tony Sarg, hired to design display windows, developed a series of large animal-shaped balloons, created by the Goodyear company. Such cartoon characters as Felix the Cat, Mickey Mouse, and others quickly joined the procession.

While originally the parade was of interest primarily to New Yorkers, the 1947 film *Miracle on 34th Street*, which including parade footage, turned the event into a national celebration.

Of course, Macy's wasn't the only sponsor of Thanksgiving Day parades. Detroit's America's Thanksgiving Day Parade is the same age; Philadelphia's 6abc Dunkin' Donuts Thanksgiving Parade (originally the Gimbels Thanksgiving Parade, sponsored by Macy's traditional department store rival) is four years older, and is the oldest Thanksgiving Day parade in the United States.

It takes 90 people to handle one of the giant balloons, and numerous safety procedures have been developed over the years in response to balloon accidents. If wind speeds are above 34 miles per hour, the balloons are removed from that year's parade.

In addition to balloons, the parade features floats, high school and college marching bands, the casts of Broadway shows, the Rockettes of Radio City Music Hall, and numerous pop singers and other celebrities. It's become a national icon, as much a part of the Thanksgiving celebration as the turkey itself.

Balloon inflation crewmembers being trained
(Photo: M. Krupnic)

Santa Claus arrives at the end of the parade

Michael Dobson

The Berners Street Hoax, by William Heath (1810)

What Happened on November 27?

From the creation of great works of engineering and art, to devastating wars and natural disasters, thousands of years of history have left their mark on each and every day of the year. Here are some important events that occurred on November 27. (Items with a photo or illustration are boxed.

1095 — The **First Crusade** is declared by Pope Urban I, initially to repel invading Turks from Anatolia, but is expanded to include the attempted Christian reconquest of Jerusalem. It succeeded for a time, but not permanently. There were nine major Crusades altogether, along with smaller ones, continuing from the 11th to the 16th centuries.

1810 — Prankster Theodore Hook perpetrates the **Berners Street hoax**. Betting a friend he could turn any house in London into the most talked-about address in town, he arranged for hundreds of chimney sweeps, bakers, fishmongers, piano deliveries, and numerous dignitaries including the Duke of York and Archbishop of Canterbury to appear at the house of Mrs. Tottenham at 54 Berners Street beginning at 5 o'clock in the morning, turning the area into utter chaos until late evening. Hook himself managed to evade detection but wisely left London for a tour of the countryside.

1868 — The 7th US Cavalry, commanded by Lieutenant Colonel George Armstrong Custer, attacked a Cheyenne winter encampment on the Washita River, an event known as the **Battle of Washita River** or the **Washita Massacre**. Custer had his men specifically target Indian noncombatants, including women and children, to force the warriors to surrender. There was a controversy at the time (continuing to this day) whether it is more accurate to call it a military victory or a massacre.

"The Seventh US Cavalry Charging into Black Kettle's Village at Daylight" (1868)

1895 — Dynamite inventor Alfred Nobel signs his last will and testament, in which he sets aside his estate to establish the **Nobel Prize.**

1945 — The Cooperative for American Remittances to Europe (CARE) is founded. Its first major project is providing food aid to post-war Europe through millions of **CARE Packages,** which could be sent to a specific person for only $10. The postage included a return receipt, allowing many people to confirm for the first time whether their loved ones had survived the war.

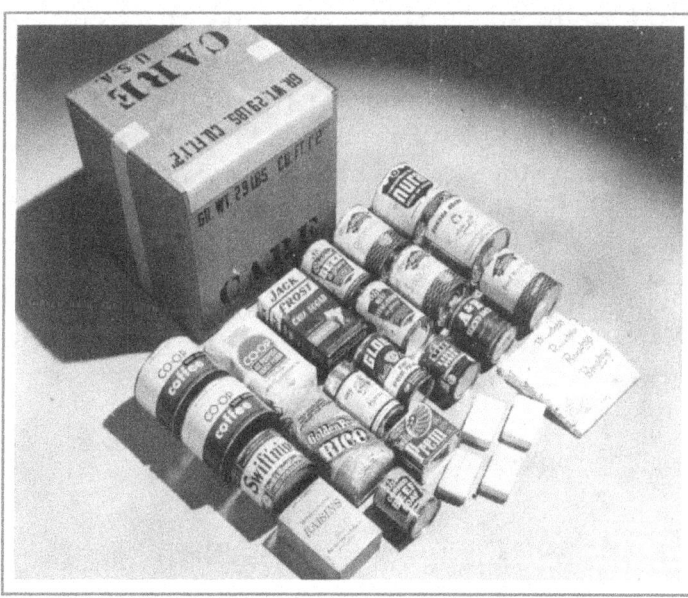

A CARE Package (German Federal Archives)

1954 — Convicted spy **Alger Hiss** is released from prison. Although Hiss denied that he had ever been a Soviet spy, and his conviction at the time was controversial, growing evidence has led to a general historical consensus that he was indeed guilty of espionage.

1968 — **Penny Ann Early**, who had already become the first licensed female jockey in the United States, becomes the **first woman to play in a professional basketball league**, appearing with the Kentucky Colonels in a game against the Los Angeles Stars.

1971 — The **Soviet Mars 2** unmanned space probe enters orbit around the planet Mars and releases a descent module. Although the parachute did not deploy and the module crashed, it is still the **first man-made object to reach the surface of Mars**.

1978 — San Francisco Mayor **George Moscone** and city supervisor **Harvey Milk**, the first openly gay person to be elected to public office in California, are **assassinated by Dan White**, another city supervisor.

Quote of the Day

"I want to do everything in the world that can be done!'

Fanny Kemble, actress and author
born November 27, 1809

Notable November 27 People

With the current world population at about seven billion people, on average about 19 million people also celebrate their birthdays on November 27 — and that isn't counting millions and millions who came before! No matter when you were born, you share your birthday with many special people whose accomplishments (and occasionally embarrassments) have been noted as part of history.

In this section, you'll meet fascinating people who share your birthday. They're organized by what they're famous for, and then in reverse chronological order from most recent to earliest. Those who are shown in photographs or artwork have a box around them. We don't have photos of everyone, so please forgive us if your favorite person is missing.

Some of these people you've heard of, others will be new to you, but they all make up an important part of the reason that November 27 is a truly special day!

Caroline Kennedy, left, with father President John F. Kennedy, 1963
(Photo: Cecil Stoughton)

Who Was Born on November 27?

Business and Industry

Cal Worthington, car dealer famous for his offbeat television commercials featuring "My Dog Spot," in which Spot was a different animal each time, but never an actual dog. His commercials were parodied in numerous films. (1920)

Kōnosuke Matsushita (松下 幸之助), founder of the Japanese consumer electronics company Panasonic, sometimes called "the god of management." (1894)

Crime and Punishment

Vito Genovese, Mafia boss, leader of the Genovese crime family. (1897)

Elizabeth Stride, believed to be one of the victims of notorious serial killer Jack the Ripper. (1843)

Government and Politics

Caroline Kennedy, daughter of President John F. Kennedy and First Lady Jacqueline Kennedy, served as United States Ambassador to Japan. (1957)

Benigno Aquino Jr., Philippine politician and husband of future president Corazon Aquino, assassinated upon his return to the Philippines after a period in exile. (1932)

Alexander Dubček, Slovakian president who attempted to reform Communist Czechoslovakia during the Prague Spring, but was forced to resign following the Warsaw Pact invasion of Czechoslovakia in 1968. (1921)

Chaim Weizmann (חיים עזריאל ויצמן), first president of Israel. (1874)

Robert Livingston, a founding father of the United States, a member of the committed that drafted the Declaration of Independence, and first Secretary of Foreign Affairs. (1746 — *O.S. November 16)

Journalism and Letters

Kevin Henkes, illustrator and writer of children's books, won a Caldecott Medal for the 2004 book *Kitten's First Full Moon.*

John McCarthy, British journalist who was one of the hostages in the Lebanon hostage crisis, held for more than five years before his release. (1956)

Marilyn Hacker, poet, translator, and critic, winner of the National Book Award and the PEN/Voelker Award. She was married to the science fiction writer Samuel R. Delany.

DRAFTING THE DECLARATION OF INDEPENDENCE.

THE COMMITTEE—FRANKLIN, JEFFERSON, ADAMS, LIVINGSTON AND SHERMAN.

Drafting the Declaration of Independence. From left to right: Benjamin Franklin, Thomas Jefferson, John Adams, **Robert Livingston**, and Roger Sherman

Gail Sheehy, author of the 1976 book *Passages,*
named by the Library of Congress as one of the ten
most influential books of our time. (1937)

James Agee, writer and critic, winner of the Pulitzer
Prize for his autobiographical novel A *Death in the
Family* and author of the classic L*et Us Now Praise
Famous Men,* considered one of the greatest literary
works of the 20th century. (1909)

L. Sprague de Camp, historian and science fiction
writer, named a Grand Master by the Science Fiction
Writers of America. (1907)

Science fiction writers Robert A. Heinlein, **L. Sprague de Camp,**
and Isaac Asimov, Philadelphia Navy Yard, 1944

Katherine Milhous, illustrator and writer, known for the Caldecott Medal-winning *The Egg Tree*. (1894)

Charles A. Beard, considered one of the most influential American historians of the early 20th century, best known for *An Economic Interpretation of the Constitution of the United States*. (1847)

Robert Lowth, bishop who wrote one of the first books on English grammar, establishing a number of rules such as not ending a sentence with a preposition. (1701)

Military and Exploration

Dora Dougherty Strother, US military pilot and human factors engineer, winner of the Amelia Earhart Award and an inductee of the Military Aviation Hall of Fame. (1921)

Masaharu Homma (本間 雅晴), Japanese general who commanded the invasion of Philippines and was hanged for war crimes related to actions of his troops during the Bataan Death March. (1887)

Georg Foster, naturalist and travel writer considered one of the founders of modern scientific travel literature, author of *A Voyage Round the World*. (1754)

Music

Jimi Hendrix, guitarist and singer-songwriter, called "arguably the greatest instrumentalist in the history of rock music" by the Rock and Roll Hall of Fame, famous for such hits as "Purple Haze" and for his performance of "The Star-Spangled Banner" at the Woodstock Festival. (1942)

The Jimi Hendrix Experience, Jimi Hendrix standing

Eddie Rabbit, crossover country singer and songwriter, known for such hits as "Suspicion" and "Every Which Way But Loose." (1941)

Performing Arts

Jaleel White, actor best known for his role as Steve Urkel on the sitcom *Family Matters.* (1976)

Samantha Harris, co-host of *Dancing with the Stars* for seven seasons. (1973)

Sharlto Copley, actor, producer, and director known for playing Murdock in the 2010 film *The A-Team,* as well as roles in *District 9, Europa Report,* and *Elysium.* (1973)

Kirk Acevedo, actor known for his roles in *Oz, Band of Brothers, Fringe,* and *12 Monkeys.* (1971)

Robin Givens, actress best known for her marriage to boxer Mike Tyson. (1964)

Fisher Stevens, actor and filmmaker who won an Academy Award in 2010 for his film *The Cove*; also appeared in such films as *Short Circuit.*

Samantha Bond, actress who played Miss Moneypenny in the James Bond films starring Pierce Brosnan, as well as Lady Painswick in the television series *Downton Abbey.* (1961)

Callie Khouri, won an Academy Award for Best Screenplay for the 1991 film *Thelma & Louise.* (1957)

Curtis Armstrong, actor known for his roles in the *Revenge of the Nerds* films, *Risky Business,* and the television series *Moonlighting.* (1953)

Kathryn Bigelow, director and producer who became the first woman to win an Academy Award for Best Director for her 2009 film *The Hurt Locker.* (1951)

James Avery, American actor who played the uncle in the Will Smith sitcom *The Fresh Prince of Bel-Air.* (1945)

Bruce Lee, actor and martial artist, founder of the Jeet Kun Do school and star of such films as 1973's *Enter the Dragon.*

Ernie Wise, English comedian best known as part of the comedy duo Morecambe and Wise. (1925)

Bruce Lee, from the TV series *The Green Hornet* (1967)

Buffalo Bob Smith, host of the children's show *Howdy Doody*, one of the most popular television shows in the United States, running from 1947 to 1960. (1917)

David Merrick, American theatrical producer and multiple Tony Award winner, whose productions include *42nd Street, Rosencrantz and Guildenstern Are Dead, Marat/Sade, Hello Dolly!, Oliver!,* and many more. (1911)

Fanny Kemble, British actress who became a popular writer, authored Journal of a Residence on a Georgia Plantation that became well known in abolitionist circles for its portrayal of slave life in the United States. (1809) *Photo page 12.*

Science and Medicine

Bill Nye the Science Guy, science educator and television presenter. (1955)

Lars Onsager, physical chemist, won the 1968 Nobel Prize in Chemistry. (1903)

Sir Charles Scott Sherrington, shared the 1932 Nobel Prize in Physiology and Medicine for his work on the function of neurons in the brain. (1857)

Anders Celsius, Swedish astronomer, physicist, and mathematician famous for developing the Celsius temperature scale. (1701)

Buffalo Bob Smith and Howdy Doody

Bill Nye the Science Guy (Photo: John F. Williams)

Sports

Ricky Carmichael, motocross racer inducted into the Motorsports Hall of Fame in 2015. (1979)

Jimmy Rollins, baseball shortstop named National League MVP in 2007. (1978)

Iván Rodríguez, baseball catcher named American League MVP in 1999 and considered one of the best defensive catchers of all time. (1971)

Larry Allen, football guard regarded as one of the physically strongest men ever to have played in the NFL; named to the Pro Football Hall of Fame. (1971)

Davey Boy Smith, professional wrestler known as "The British Bulldog," held numerous titles in the World Wrestling Federation. (1962)

Ken O'Brien, football quarterback for the New York Jets and Philadelphia Eagles, named to the College Football Hall of Fame in 1997. (1960)

Mike Scioscia, named American League Manager of the Year in 2002 and 2009 for his work with the Los Angeles Angels. (1958)

Henry Carr, track and field athlete and football player who won two Gold Medals at the 1964 Summer Olympics. (1941)

Chick Hearn, sportscaster known as the play-by-play announcer for the Los Angeles Lakers, created such phrases as "slam dunk," "air ball," and "no harm, no foul." (1916)

Ted Husing, pioneering sportscaster who helped lay the groundwork for the structure and pace of modern sports reporting, second inductee into the National Sportscasters and Sportswriters Association Hall of Fame. (1901)

1964 Tokyo Olympics Medal Ceremony with **Henry Carr** (center), Paul Drayton (left), and Edwin Roberts (right)

The Eddystone Lighthouse, designed and built by Henry
Winstanley, who died there on November 27, 1703

Who Died on November 27?

Business and Engineering

Robert Cade, physician and inventor who led the development of Gatorade. (2007)

Basil Zaharoff, international arms dealer and one of the world's richest men; known as the "Merchant of Death" for such acts as selling arms to opposing sides in the same conflict and for delivering fake or faulty products. (1936)

Clement Studebaker, co-founder of Studebaker Corporation, originally known for building Conestoga wagons and later automobiles. (1901)

Andrew Meikle, Scottish engineer who invented the threshing machine. (1811)

Henry Winstanley, designed and built the first Eddystone lighthouse, which he believed to be so safe that he wished it would be inside it during "the greatest storm there ever was." He got his wish; he was in the lighthouse when it was destroyed during a great storm. (1703)

Crime and Punishment

Baby Face Nelson, bank robber known for his partnership with John Dillinger, named Public Enemy #1 for killing more FBI agents in the line of duty than any other person. (1901)

Baby Face Nelson

Government and Politics

V. P. Singh, prime minister of India. (2008)

Journalism and Letters

P. D. James, crime writer known for her novels featuring police commander Adam Dalgliesh. She was also Baroness James of Holland Park and a life peer in the House of Lords. (2014)

Bebe Moore Campbell, author of the New York *Times* bestsellers *Brothers and Sisters, Singing in the Comeback Choir,* and *What You Owe Me,* winner of the NAACP Image Award for Literature. (2006)

Elizabeth Gray Vining, librarian and author who won the Newberry Award for her children's book *Adam of the Road;* tutored future Japanese emperor Akihito in English. (1999)

Ross McWhirter, co-founder of the *Guinness Book of World Records.* (1975)

Eugene O'Neill, American playwright and Nobel laureate, best known for his play *Long Day's Journey into Night.* (1953)

Alexandre Dumas, fils, author of such novels as *La Dame aux Camélia*s, son of the author Alexandre Dumas, père, who wrote *The Three Musketeers.* (1895)

Horace, Roman lyric poet and soldier. (8 BCE)

Music

Lotte Lenya, singer and actress known for her interpretations of songs written by her husband Kurt Weill, including "Mack the Knife," famously covered by Bobby Darrin (who mentions her as "Miss Lotte Lenya" in his performance). She received an Academy Award nomination for her role in 1961's *The Roman Spring of Mrs. Stone,* and is also remembered for playing Rosa Klebb in the 1963 James Bond film *From Russia With Love.* (1981)

Arthur Honegger, Swiss composer, known particularly for his orchestral work *Pacific 231,* inspired by the sound of a steam locomotive. (1955)

Performing Arts

Ken Russell, director of the Academy Award winning *Women in Love, The Who's Tommy, Altered States,* and many other films. (2011)

Irvin Kershner, director of *The Empire Strikes Back, Never Say Never Again,* and *RoboCop 2.* (2010)

Billie Bird, actress known for her roles in *Sixteen Candles, Home Alone,* and numerous television shows. (2002)

David White, best known for playing Larry Tate on the sitcom *Bewitched.* (1990)

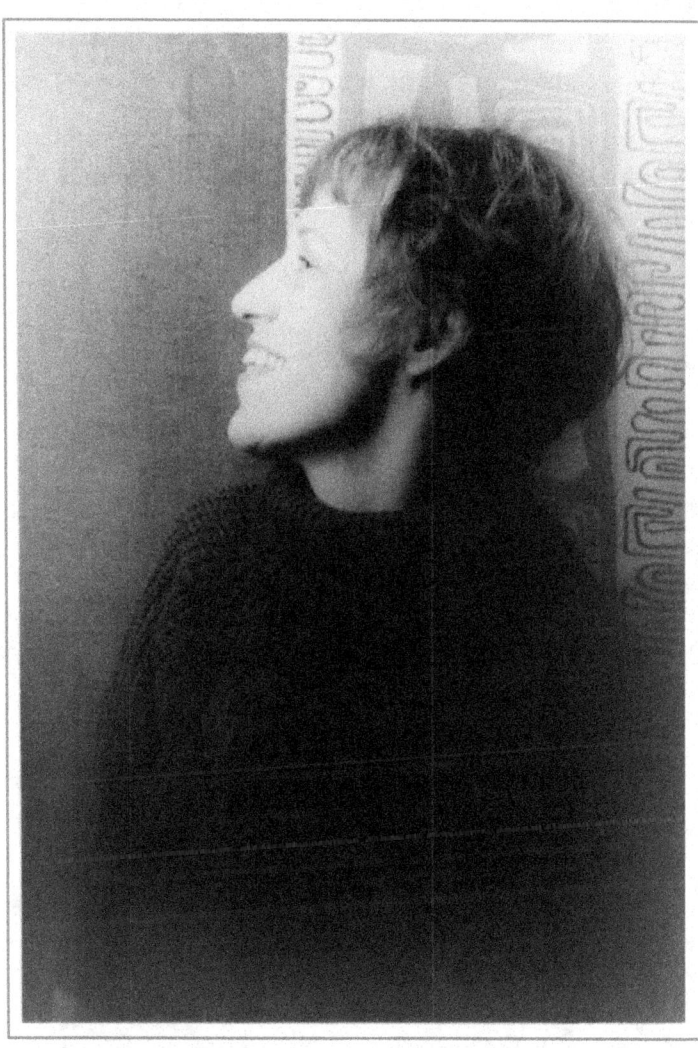

Lotte Lenya (Photo: Carl Van Vechten)

John Carradine, American actor known for roles in horror films, Westerns, and Shakespeare; patriarch of the Carradine family of actors. (1988)

Evelyn Preer, African-American actress and singer; first black actress to become a celebrity, known in the black community as "The First Lady of the Screen." (1932)

Science and Mathematics

Ada Lovelace, Countess of Lovelace, English mathematician known for her work on Charles Babbage's mechanical general-purpose computer. She developed the first algorithm to be carried out by a machine, making her the first computer programmer. She was the daughter of the poet Lord Byron, and the programming language Ada is named for her. (1852)

Sports

Bill Willis, football defensive lineman, one of the first African Americans to play professional football. Member of the Pro Football Hall of Fame and the College Football Hall of Fame. (2007)

Sean Taylor, Washington Redskins free safety known as the "Meast," a portmanteau word meaning "half man, half beast." (2007)

Portrait of Ada Lovelace, by Margaret Sarah Carpenter (1836)

Len Shackleton, English footballer known as the "Clown Prince of Soccer." (2000)

Buck Leonard, Negro League first baseman elected to the Baseball Hall of Fame, ranked 47 on the 100 Greatest Baseball Players list by *The Sporting News.* (1997)

Helene Madison, American swimmer who won three gold medals in the 1932 Summer Olympics, named to the International Swimming Hall of Fame and the US Olympic Hall of Fame. (1970)

Helene Madison (left) at the 1932 Olympics with fellow Olympian and future Tarzan Johnny Weissmuller

Quote of the Day

"Enjoy the present smiling hour
And put it out of Fortune's power."

Horace, Roman poet and soldier
died November 27, 8 BCE

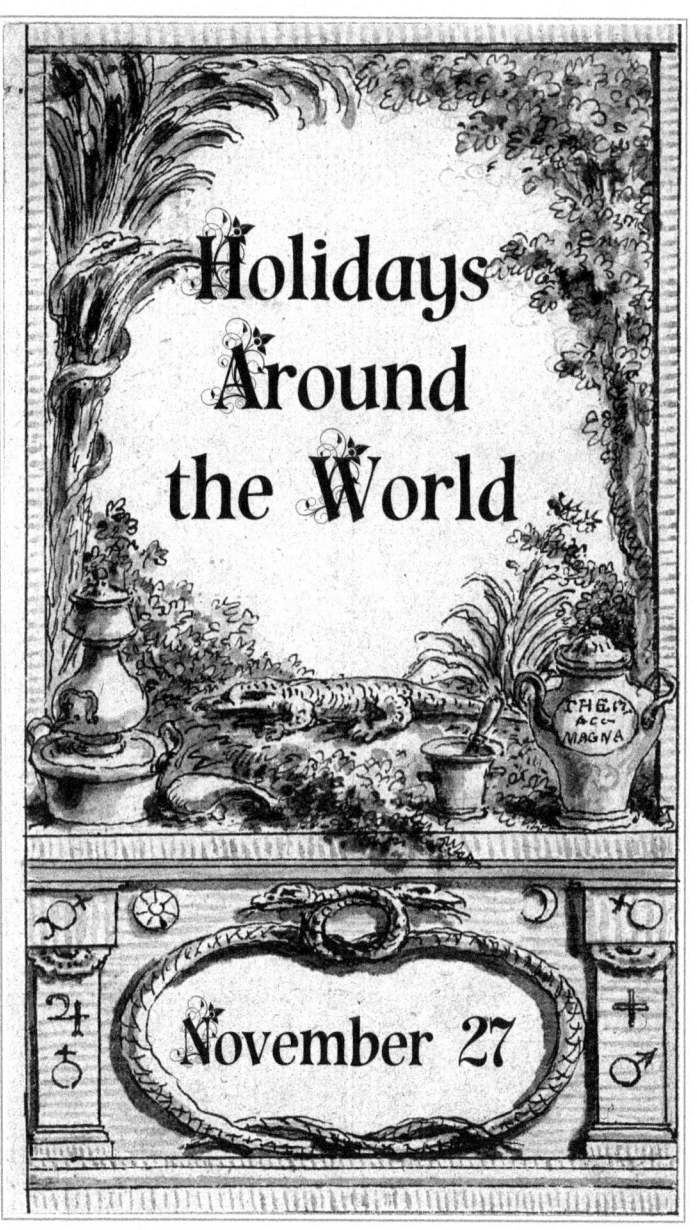

Holidays Around the World

THEM ACC MAGNA

November 27

Detail from "The First Thanksgiving," by Jean Leon Gerome Ferris

Thanksgiving

Ceremonies of giving thanks are part of many religions and many cultures. Many such festivals were held around harvest time. In some countries, the United States and Canada among them, a formal Thanksgiving Day for the nation has become a major annual holiday.

A Brief History of Thanksgiving

The origins of Thanksgiving Day in the United States and Canada trace back to the English Reformation, which instituted special Days of Thanksgiving to celebrate such events as the British victory against the Spanish Armada. One such Thanksgiving, begun in 1606, turned into the British Guy Fawkes Day.

It's unclear which Thanksgiving Day came first. Some trace the first Canadian Thanksgiving to 1578 and the explorer Martin Frobisher. In the United States, the origin of Thanksgiving is generally traced to a Pilgrim feast in 1621. As in England, Thanksgiving wasn't an automatic annual event, but happened only when declared by royal governors and later by the Continental Congress. Some Thanksgiving Days were celebrated only in a single state; others nationwide.

In both countries, Thanksgiving slowly became a standard public holiday. Canada's official

Thanksgiving Day *(Jour de l'action de grâce)* began in 1872, though it wasn't until 1957 that it settled on its current date of the second Monday of October. *(October 8 through October 14, same day as Columbus Day in the US.)*

In the United States, each state set its own Thanksgiving Day, but by the beginning of the 19th century, it was mostly on the final Thursday of November. Abraham Lincoln made it official in 1863. In 1941, however, Congress changed the date to make Thanksgiving the *fourth* Thursday of November rather than the *final* one, because some years that would leave too few days for Christmas shopping. That's why in the United States Thanksgiving Day can fall on any day from *November 22 to November 28.*

Thanksgiving in North America

Although Thanksgiving is often celebrated with prayers and proclamations, it isn't a formal religious holiday and so most rituals are secular in nature. North American celebrations normally include a large family dinner, with turkey as the traditional featured dish.

Thanksgiving dinner extends to charity as well, with many volunteering to make and serve dinner to those in need. There are several major parades, with the Macy's Thanksgiving Day Parade the best known in the US, and the Kitchener-Waterloo Oktoberfest parade in Canada. And, of course, there's football.

A Thanksgiving dream from *Little Nemo in Slumberland,* by Winsor McCay (1905)

Families often get together, making the Thanksgiving holidays one of the busiest travel periods of the year, especially in the US.

Thanksgiving in Other Countries

Different versions of Thanksgiving Day can be found around the world.

Some places have a Thanksgiving Day connected to the North American traditions. The Pieterskirk (St. Peter's Church) in Dutch city of Leiden has a nondenominational religious service on *the morning of the American Thanksgiving* because many of the Pilgrims had lived in Leiden, and had recorded marriages, births, and deaths in the Pieterskerk (St. Peter's Church).

While Australia as a whole doesn't celebrate Thanksgiving, the external Australian territory Norfolk Island does. American whaling ships brought the celebration to that island, though they celebrate it on the last Wednesday of November. (*November 24 to November 30*).

The Philippines adopted Thanksgiving when it was an American colony, but the tradition eventually faded out.

Liberia, colonized by freed black slaves from the United States, celebrates its Thanksgiving on the first Thursday of November (*November 1-7*).

In the Caribbean, Grenada celebrates Thanksgiving Day on *October 25*, the anniversary of the US-led invasion of the island in 1983 that deposed the then-current government. Saint Lucia celebratess the *first Monday in October (October 1-7)*.

In the United Kingdom, there is a Harvest Festival of Thanksgiving, but that does not have a fixed date. It's traditionally held on or near the Sunday of the harvest moon that occurs closest to the autumnal equinox, which essentially means *sometime in late September or early October,* usually close to Canadian Thanksgiving. Harvest festivals are celebrated in many countries; a complete list can be found on Wikipedia.

Thanksgiving Greetings

Thanksgiving Day is here again.
And come this year to crown:
Ok pray receive my wholesome wishes,
For well prepared Thanksgiving Dishes.

Germany holds religious ceremonies associated with *Erntedankfest,* in early October. Japan has a Labor Thanksgiving Day (勤労感謝の日, or *Kinrō Kansha no Hi*), established during the American post-World War II occupation, which commemorates labor and production and giving one another thanks. It comes from an early celebration that honored hard work.

Whatever and however you give thanks, a very happy Thanksgiving to one and all!

Michael Dobson

Detail from "Pairie Indian Encampment" by John Mix Stanley
for Native American Heritage Day

Holidays Around the World

If you're looking for a reason to take your special day off, you should know that every single day is a holiday somewhere in the world! Here's what you can celebrate on November 27!

General Events

Black Friday (United States, unofficial)

"Black Friday" is the unofficial nickname for the first day of the Christmas shopping season, which is also the day after Thanksgiving, because most people have it off. There are numerous sales and crowds in shopping centers everywhere. (*varies November 23-29*)

Maaveerar Nal (Great Heroes' Day)

The remembrance day of Maaveerar Nal is observed by the Sri Lankan Tamil people to commemorate the deaths of those who fought for the Liberation Tigers of Tamil Eelam.

Native American Heritage Day (United States)

Native American Heritage Day was established by Congress in 2008. It is celebrated the day after Thanksgiving. (*varies November 23-29*)

Teacher's Day (Spain)

Many nations have a Teacher's Day to appreciate educators. In Spain, Teacher's Day is celebrated on November 27 each year.

Food Holidays

In the United States, almost every day of the year is dedicated to a particular food. (Some other countries do this also, but not every day.) Sponsored by manufacturers, retailers, farmers, or simply fans, these days are often proclaimed by the President, Congress, state governors, or mayors. Given that there are more different foods than days of the year, some days honor more than one kind of food!

November 27 is **National Bavarian Cream Pie Day.** According to Foodimentary, bavarian cream was originally a French or German cold dessert of egg custard mixed with whipped cream. Before the invention of refrigeration, making bavarian cream was quite a feat!

In addition, the entire month of November is used to celebrate numerous foods. Here's a list of what to eat in the month of November!

- National Fun With Fondue Month
- National Georgia Pecan Month
- National Peanut Butter Lover's Month
- National Pepper Month
- National Pomegranate Month
- National Raisin Bread Month
- Sweet Potato Awareness Month
- Vegan Month

Christian Feast Days and Holidays

Advent Sunday

The first day of the liturgical year and the beginning of the season of Advent, is Advent Sunday, celebrated on the fourth Sunday before Christmas Day. It can fall on any date between November 27 and December 3.

Saint Feast Days

Each day in the year is considered a feast day for one or more saints. They are somewhat different in western Christianity (Catholicism and many forms of Protestantism) and in eastern (Orthodox) Christianity. There are many others; this is a selection.

In *Western Christianity*, Barlaam and Josaphat, Congar of Congresbury, Facundus and Primitivus, Francis Fasani, Humilis of Bisignano, Our Lady of the Miraculous Medal, and Virgilius of Salzburg are commemorated on November 27.

In *Eastern Orthodox Christianity*, it is also the commemoration of saints John Angeloptes, Seachnall, Severinus, Gallgo, Bilhildis, and Apollinaris, as well as Saint James of Rostov and Saint Damaskinos the Studite. (These are observed on November 14 by "Old Calendarists.")

Honorary Months

Presidents, Congresses, and nations around the world issue proclamations recognizing particular months to honor certain causes. These events generally fall in November, though honorary months do come and go. Holidays established by states and nonprofit organizations are listed if verified. If not otherwise specified, all months are US. There is some variation from year to year; some celebratory months get added and others get dropped. Two places to get up to date information are the current edition of *Chase's Calendar of Events* or the website Brownielocks (www.brownielocks.com).

- Adopt a Turkey Month
- Aviation History Month
- Epilepsy Awareness Month
- Historic Bridge Awareness Month
- Military Family Appreciation Month
- National Adoption Month
- National Diabetes Month
- National Family Literacy Month
- National Hospice Month
- National Memoir Writing Month
- National Novel Writing Month
- World Sponge Month

Moveable and Multi-Day Events

Some events take place over a specific week or time period. Start and finish dates may vary from year to year. Some events occur on different days each year (such as "fourth Saturday of a month"). These events sometimes take place on this day.

Week Beginning the Sunday Before Thanksgiving

- International Bible Week

Week that Ends on Thanksgiving Day

- National Farm-City Week

Week Including Thanksgiving Day

- National Family Week
- National Games Week

Day After Thanksgiving

- Flossing Day
- National Day of Listening
- You're Welcomegiving Day

Saturday After Thanksgiving

- Small Business Saturday

Quote of the Day

"It was one of those perfect English autumnal days which occur more frequently in memory than in life.""

P. D. James, crime writer
died November 27, 2014

About the Month of November

November, from the *Brevarium Grimani* (c.1510)

November: The Eleventh Month

When shrieked
The bleak November winds, and smote the woods,
And the brown fields were herbless, and the shades
That met above the merry rivulet
Were spoiled, I sought, I loved them still; they seemed
Like old companions in adversity.

William Cullen Bryant, A Winter Piece

In Latin, *novem* means "nine," so it may seem strange that November is the eleventh month of the year. The original Roman calendar started in March, making November indeed the ninth month. No one is completely sure when the start of the year was moved to January, but the traditional name of November stuck.

In the northern hemisphere, November is a month in late autumn. In the southern hemisphere, November is in the springtime. May is its opposite month; spring in the north and fall in the south.

If it's not a Leap Year, November always starts on the same day of the week as February. If it is a leap year, November starts on the same day of the week as March.

November in Other Cultures

The month of November has different names in different languages. Some nations use calendars other than the Gregorian, and their months may overlap with November. In lunar-based calendars, such as the Islamic calendar, months move through the seasons. Still, many languages often have a word for November itself.

Arabic: نوفمبر (Nūfambar)

Chinese and Japanese: 十一月

Croatian: Studeni

Czech and Polish: Listopad

Finnish: Marraskuu

Greek: Νοέμβριος

Hebrew: נובמבר

Hindi: नवंबर

Old English: Blōtmōnaþ

Russian: ноябрь

November Sayings and Superstitions

Here are some sayings and superstitions associated with the month of November

- "A November bride will be liberal and kind, but sometimes cold."
- "Married in veils of November mist / Fortune your wedding ring has kissed."
- "If you wed in bleak November, only joys will come, remember."

November, by Eugène Grasset

November Symbols

Birthstone: Topaz (primarily yellow), and citrine (left). Topaz is associated with strength, tenacity, dedication and resilience. Citrine is supposed to encourage vitality and promote good health.

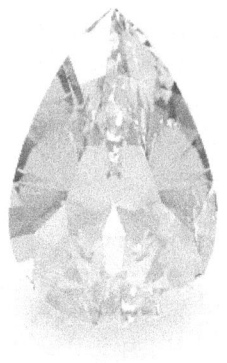

Citrine

Birth Flower: Chrysanthemum. The Chrysanthemum is associated with compassion, friendship,and joy. Red is for love, white for innocence, and yellow for unrequited love.

Chrysanthemums, by Claude Monet

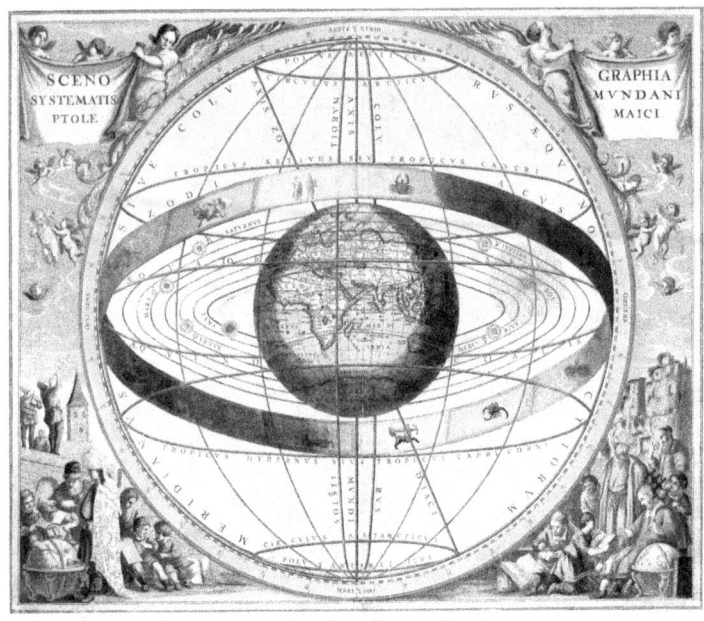

Scenography of the Ptolemaic Cosmography, by Johannes van Loon, based on Andreas Cellarius's *Harmonia Macrocosmica,* 1660

November 27 Zodiac Signs

From the perspective of someone on Earth, the Sun appears to move through the sky throughout the year, along a path astronomers call the *ecliptic plane*. The ecliptic plane is divided into twelve constellations, known as the zodiac, based on traditionally observed patterns of stars. On your birthday, you can't see your constellation, because it's in the daytime sky.

The zodiac was first developed by Babylonian astronomers about 2,500 years ago. Because they were unaware that the Earth wobbles like a spinning top (known as *precession*), they didn't make allowance for the fact that the Sun's path through the zodiac changes over time.

That means there are now two sets of dates for your birth sign. The *tropical dates* are the original Babylonian dates; the *sidereal dates* tell you where the Sun actually appears as it moves along its annual path.

For November 27, the tropical signs is **Sagittarius** and the sidereal sign is **Scorpio**.

Sagittarius

Tropical November 23 to December 21
Sidereal December 16 to January 14

The centaur (half-man, half-horse) Chiron was
famous as a healer and as an archer. He tutored
Achilles, Jason (of Argonaut fame), and Hercules.
Unfortunately for Chiron, Hercules accidentally shot
him with an arrow that had been dipped in hydra
poison. He was unable to find a cure, so gave up his
immortality to free Prometheus, and died. In
recognition of his sacrifice, Zeus placed him among
the stars.

In astrology, Sagittarians are known for their
independence and craving for adventure and
excitement. They are encouraging and kind, but
sometimes lack commitment. They are supposed to
be compatible with Aries, Leo, and Libra, but not
with Taurus, Scorpio, or Capricorn.

Scorpio

Tropical October 23 to November 21
Sidereal November 16 to December 15

Scorpio, the Scorpion, appears in the Greek myth of the hunter Orion. Because Orion had touched the robes of the goddess Artemis, in revenge, the goddess had the scorpion kill Orion. As a reward, she placed the scorpion in the sky, where it chases Orion through the eternal night.

Scorpio is a fire sign, and people born under this sign are supposed to be determined, reserved, loyal, and secretive. Scorpios are supposed to be compatible with the water signs of Pisces and Capricorn.

Illustration by Edward Penfield

What Day of the Week is November 27?

On what day of the week does November 27 fall?

Surprisingly, this isn't an easy question. Because the calendar year is 365 days long (366 in leap years), it doesn't divide evenly by the seven days of the week.

Also, the Earth goes around the Sun in about 365-1/4 days, so a calendar tends to drift over time. That's why the same date falls on different weekdays in different years.

This is made even more complicated by a change in calendars that took place in 1582. Our modern calendar has its roots in ancient Rome, in a calendar reform conducted by Julius Caesar. Caesar commissioned mathematicians to attack the problem, and they came up with the idea of leap years, and thus standardized the calendar for centuries to come. This was called the Julian calendar.

Over time, however, the small errors in Caesar's calculation compounded. That's why Pope Gregory XIII commissioned the Gregorian calendar, used in most of the world today. Some countries converted in 1582, when the calendar was first developed; some converted later; other still haven't changed.

Gregorian and Julian aren't the only types of calendars. The Hebrew year, the Islamic year, and many other calendars are used in different parts of the world and among different people.

You can convert Gregorian dates to other calendars, including the Hebrew calendar, the Islamic calendar, and even the Mayan calendar by visiting the Fourmilab Calendar Converter at http://www.fourmilab.ch/documents/calendar/.

Chinese calendar systems are quite complex and have changed several times; a full discussion is far beyond the scope of this book. If you're interested, you can find information here: http://www.hermetic.ch/cal_stud/chinese_cal.htm.

On Names and Dates

Historians use "CE" (Common Era) and "BCE" (Before the Common Era) instead of the more common "AD" (Anno Domini, or Year of Our Lord) and "BC" (Before Christ), reflecting the fact that the year-numbering system established by the Gregorian calendar is used throughout the world in many countries not culturally Christian.

The CE/BCE designation dates back to at least 1708, and has been adopted as a standard by the United Nations and the Universal Postal Union. Because this series of books covers events and people of all nations and cultures, we use the CE/BCE terms.

The abbreviation "O.S." ("Old Style") on some dates refers to the fact that the Russian Empire did not switch from the Julian to the Gregorian calendar at the same time as the rest of Europe, and therefore some figures and events have two dates.

Also, in the Julian calendar in England in the 16th century, the year began on March 25 rather than January 1. To avoid confusion with Gregorian dates, dates between January and March were often written using both years.

People and events whose original names are not in the Western alphabet have their native names (where possible) in the appropriate script shown in parenthesis. If you are using an e-reader to access an electronic version of this book, all characters don't always display on all devices.

A 50-year brass perpetual calendar.

Quote of the Day

"Time is an illusion, lunchtime doubly so."

Douglas Adams,
from *The Hitchhiker's Guide to the Galaxy*

Notes and Credits

Timespinner
Press

Cartoon by John T. McCutcheon

Copyright, Credit, and Contact

Follow Us

Our blog "This Day in History" (http://timespinnerpress.com/this-day-in-history/) features short articles on events and people associated with each day, and updates several times each week. Also subscribe to the "Quote of the Day" at http://timespinnerpress.com/quote-of-the-day/. You can get daily links by following us on Facebook at TimespinnerPress, or on Twitter as @sidewisethinker.

Contact Us

Find an error or a format problem? Want information about the series, about us, or about when the volume for your special day might be available? Please email us at editor@timespinnerpress.com. (We also take requests if your special day isn't yet complete. Please give us at least six weeks' notice if possible.)

Sources

We owe a great debt to Wikipedia, which is our first stop for research. We attempt to make independent confirmation of all important dates and facts through a variety of other sources.

Other sources we frequently use include the Library of Congress; "on this day" listings from *Encyclopedia Britannica,* the *New York Times,* and the BBC; Omniglot for the names of months in other languages; *Chase's Calendar of Events;* and, of course, the always essential Google.

All art and photographs are either in the public domain, used under a Creative Commons license, or with a "fair use" justification, and most frequently come from Wikimedia Commons and the Library of Congress Prints and Photographs Division.

Attribution is provided where possible, or as requested by the copyright owner, or when there is particular historical significance, listed below. For information about any particular illustration or photograph, please contact us.

Credits

1. The cover photograph of the 2008 Macy's Thanksgiving Day Parade is by "Ben+Sam," and is used here under CC BY-SA 2.0.

2. The illustration of the month of November used on the back cover is from the French Gothic illuminated manuscript *Les Très Riches Heures du duc de Berry* by the Limbourg Brothers, Jean Colombe, and an intermediate painter whose name is lost to history.

3. The box graphic used on the first page is from a 1916 pamphlet entitled "Divorce versus Democracy" authored by G. K. Chesterton, originally published in London by the Society of St. Peter and St. Paul. It is in the public domain in the US because it was published prior to 1923, and is in the public domain in all countries (including the country of origin) in which the copyright time is the author's life plus 70 years or less.

4. The graphic design for the section pages in this book is from a design originally created for a pharmacy label. It is from Wellcome Images (ICV No 11073, photo V0010813), and is used here under CC BY-SA 4.0.

5. The 2007 photograph of the Mr. Potato Head balloon is by Ian Gampon, and is used here under CC BY-SA 2.0.

6. The 2006 photograph of balloon inflation crew members being trained was taken by M. Krupnick, who released it into the public domain without conditions.

7. The 2008 photograph of Santa Claus at the Macy's Thanksgiving Day Parade was taken by T. Weber and is used here under CC BY-SA 2.0. It has been cropped.

8. The 1810 caricature of the Berners Street Hoax is by William Heath, and is in the public domain because its copyright has expired.

9. The uncredited 1868 engraving "The Seventh US Cavalry Charging into Black Kettle's Village at Daylight" first appeared in the December 19, 1868, issue of Harper's Weekly, and is in the public domain because its copyright has expired. The image is available from the Library of Congress, LC-USZ62-117247.

10. The 1948 photograph of a CARE Package is courtesy of the German Federal Archive (Bundesarchiv Bild 183-S1207-502), and is used here under CC BY-SA 3.0 Germany.

11. The 1873 engraving of Fanny Kemble is in the public domain because its copyright has expired. It is available from the Library of Congress (cph.3b17325).

12. The 1963 photograph of President John F. Kennedy and his daughter Caroline was taken by official White House photographer Cecil Stoughton. It is in the public domain as a work created by an employee of the US federal government as part of that person's official duties. It has been cropped for this use.

13. The engraving "Drafting the Declaration of Independence" is by Alonzo Chappel, and is in the public domain because its copyright has expired. It is the the collection of the US National Archives, ARC 513332.

14. The 1944 photograph of Robert Heinlein, L. Sprague de Camp, and Isaac Asimov at the Philadelphia Navy Yard is in the public domain as a work created by an employee of the US Navy as part of that person's official duties.

15. The 1968 Reprise Records publicity photograph of the Jimi Hendrix Experience is in the public domain because it was first published in the United States between 1923 and 1977 without a copyright notice. Traditionally, publicity photographs are not copyrighted because of the way in which they are intended to be used.

16. The 1967 ABC publicity photograph of Bruce Lee from the TV series *The Green Hornet* is in the public domain because it

was first published in the United States between 1923 and 1977 without a copyright notice. Traditionally, publicity photographs are not copyrighted because of the way in which they are intended to be used.

17. The 1972 portrait of Buffalo Bob Smith and Howdy Doody is from the collection of the State Library and Archives of Florida. No known copyright restrictions exist for the use of this photograph.

18. The 2011 photograph of Bill Nye is in the public domain as an image released by the US Navy. (ID 110505-N-PO-203-205).

19. The 1964 photograph of a medal awards ceremony at the Tokyo Olympics is by Mario De Biassi/Georgio Lotti for Mondadori Publishers. It is in the public domain in its country of origin (Italy) because its term of copyright has expired according to the Law for the Protection of Copyright and Neighbouring Rights n.633, 22 April 1941.

20. The engraving of Winstanley's Lighthouse at the Eddystone was created circa 1860 and is in the public domain because its copyright has expired.

21. The photograph of Baby Face Nelson is in the public domain as a work created by an employee of the US Federal Bureau of Investigation.

22. The 1962 photograph of Lotte Lenya was taken by Carl Van Vechten and is part of the Van Vechten Collection at the Library of Congress Prints and Photographs Division (reproduction III TT 14). It is in the public domain according to the terms of the deed of gift, but the estate has requested proper credit to the photographer.

23. The 1836 portrait of Ada Lovelace by Margaret Sarah Carpenter is in the public domain because its copyright has expired. The original is part of the Government Art Collection at 10 Downing Street, London.

24. The 1932 photograph of Helene Madison and Johnny Weissmuller at the Olympic Games is in the public domain because its copyright has expired and its author is anonymous.

25. The painting "The First Thanksgiving" by Jean Leon Gerome Farris was created between 1912 and 1915 as part of the series *The Pageant of a Nation*, and this image is available

from the Library of Congress Prints and Photographs Division under digital ID cph.3g04961 It is in the public domain because its copyright has expired. The image has been cropped

26. The 1905 Thanksgiving comic strip from *Little Nemo in Slumberland* by Winsor McCay is in the public domain in the United States because it was published or registered with the US Copyright Office before January 1, 1923.

27. The 1910 Thanksgiving postcard was published by Wolf & Co., New York. It is in the public domain because its copyright has expired.

28. The painting "Prairie Indian Encampment" by John Mix Stanley is in the collection of the Detroit Institute of Arts, and is in the public domain because its copyright has expired. It has been cropped.

29. The painting "November" is from the *Brevarium Grimani*, circa 1510, and is in the public domain because its copyright has expired.

30. The 1896 postcard "November" by Eugène Grasset is in the public domain because its copyright has expired.

31. The photograph of a citrine is by Les Facettes and is used here under CC BY-SA 3.0.

32. The 1882 painting of chrysanthemums by Claude Monet is in the public domain because its copyright has expired. The painting is in the collection of the Metropolitan Museum of Art, New York.

33. The celestial sphere is from *Scenography of the Ptolemaic Cosmography*, by Johannes van Loon, based on Andreas Cellarius's *Harmonia Macrocosmica*, 1660. It is in the public domain because its copyright has expired.

34. The 1906 automobile calendar is by Edward Penfield, and is in the collection of the Library of Congress Prints and Photographs Division. It is in the public domain because its copyright has expired.

35. The 50-year perpetual calendar photograph is in the public domain.

36. The cartoon by John T. McCutcheon is from his 1905 collection *The Mysterious Stranger and Other Cartoons by John T. McCutcheon*. It is in the public domain because its copyright has expired.

License Description and Terms

Aside from material purely in the public domain, photographs and other material in this book are used under specific licenses permitting free use, usually with an attribution requirement. For full text and terms of these licenses, click or enter the appropriate links below. If you believe there is an error in the copyright status or attribution of any of these images, please email us.

- Creative Commons Attribution 2.0 Generic (CC-BY 2.0): http://creativecommons.org/licenses/by/2.0/deed.en

- Creative Commons Attribution-Share Alike 3.0 Generic (CC-BY-SA 3.0): http://creativecommons.org/licenses/by-sa/3.0/

- Creative Commons Attribution-Share Alike 2.5 Generic (CC-BY-SA 2.5): http://creativecommons.org/licenses/by-sa/2.5/deed.en

- Creative Commons Attribution-Share Alike 2.0 Generic (CC-BY-SA 2.0): http://creativecommons.org/licenses/by/2.0/deed.en

- Creative Commons Attribution-Share Alike 1.0 Generic (CC-BY-SA 1.0): http://creativecommons.org/licenses/by-sa/1.0/deed.en

- CC0 1.0 Universal (CC0 1.0) Public Domain Dedication (CC0 1.0) http://creativecommons.org/publicdomain/zero/1.0/deed.en

- GNU Free Documentation License (GFDL): http://en.wikipedia.org/wiki/Wikipedia:Text_of_the_GNU_Free_Documentation_License

Timespinner
Press

Other Books from Timespinner Press

The Story of a Special Day
Michael Dobson

A series of (eventually) 366 volumes covering everything that happened on your special day! Events, births, deaths, quotes, holidays, and much more. It's like a birthday card they'll never throw away!

US$7.95 print/US$2.99 ebook.

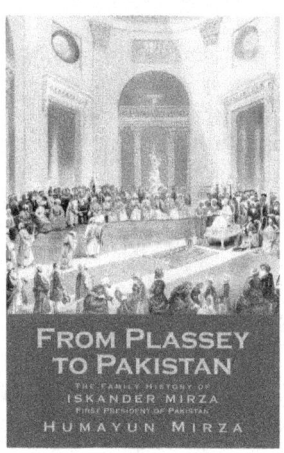

From Plassey to Pakistan
Humayun Mirza

The history of British Colonial India and the formation of Pakistan from the unique perspective of the son of Pakistan's first president and last of the royal line of Bengal, Bihar, and Orissa! This unique historical document tells the inside story of this distinguished family, including the detailed story of the coup that toppled his father from power!

US$27.95 print

Michael Dobson

A Whole New Navy: America's War in the Pacific

Miles Durr

The most comprehensive and detailed description of America's naval war in the Pacific ever—every battle, every ship, every task force and every task group from Pearl Harbor through the Japanese surrender! A must-have for the collection of every World War II buff!

US$29.95 print

Improbable History: The Weird, the Obscure, and the Strangely Important

edited by Michael Dobson

From the birth of Western civilization to the rescue of Apollo 13, from the Leaning Tower of Pisa to Florence's Duomo, history has often turned on small, improbable details. Whatever happened to the ancient Samaritan people? Why did a fortuitous rainstorm allow the British to conquer India? How did an air raid in Italy lead to the development of chemotherapy? What happened when Albert Einstein met Adolf Hitler on the streets of Berlin? How did the Japanese manage to attack the US mainland using balloons? A cast of award-winning writers tackle some of the strangest tales in history!

US$19.95 print